Association American Art

Modern Paintings

The Private Collections of Walter Bowne, William H. Shaw, William T. Evans, and the Late Bernhard Stern

Association American Art

Modern Paintings
The Private Collections of Walter Bowne, William H. Shaw, William T. Evans, and the Late Bernhard Stern

ISBN/EAN: 9783744677332

Printed in Europe, USA, Canada, Australia, Japan

Cover: Foto ©Thomas Meinert / pixelio.de

More available books at **www.hansebooks.com**

CATALOGUE

OF THE

PRIVATE COLLECTION

OF

MODERN PAINTINGS

BELONGING TO

MR. WALTER BOWNE

OF

FLUSHING, LONG ISLAND

TO BE ABSOLUTELY SOLD BY AUCTION

ON WEDNESDAY EVENING, MARCH 5TH

AT THE AMERICAN ART GALLERIES

No. 6 EAST 23D STREET, MADISON SQUARE

WHERE THE PAINTINGS ARE NOW ON PUBLIC
EXHIBITION

THOMAS E. KIRBY, AUCTIONEER

AMERICAN ART ASSOCIATION, MANAGERS

NEW YORK
1890

CONDITIONS OF SALE.

1. The highest bidder to be the Buyer, and if any dispute arise between two or more Bidders, the Lot so in dispute shall be immediately put up again and re-sold.

2. The Purchasers to give their names and addresses, and to pay down a cash deposit, or the whole of the Purchase-money, *if required*, in default of which the Lot or Lots so purchased to be immediately put up again and re-sold.

3. The Lots to be taken away at the Buyer's expense and Risk on the morning following each session of the Sale, between 9 and 12 o'clock, and the remainder of the Purchase-money to be absolutely paid, or otherwise settled for to the satisfaction of the Auctioneer, on or before delivery; in default of which the undersigned will not hold himself responsible if the Lots be lost, stolen, damaged, or destroyed, but they will be left at the sole risk of the Purchaser.

4. The sale of any painting is not to be set aside on account of any error in the description. All are exposed for Public Exhibition one or more days, and are sold just as they are without recourse.

5. To prevent inaccuracy in delivery and inconvenience in the settlement of the purchases, no Lot can, on any account, be removed during the Sale.

6. Upon failure to comply with the above conditions, the money deposited in part payment shall be forfeited ; all Lots uncleared within the time aforesaid shall be re-sold by public or private Sale, without further notice, and the deficiency (if any) attending such re-sale, shall be made good by the defaulter at this Sale, together with all charges attending the same. This Condition is without prejudice to the right of the Auctioneer to enforce the contract made at this Sale, without such re-sale, if he thinks fit.

THOMAS E. KIRBY, Auctioneer.

INDEX TO ARTISTS REPRESENTED,

TOGETHER WITH BIOGRAPHICAL NOTES, LISTS OF HONORS, AND OTHER INFORMATION.

BEAUQUESNE (WILFRID CONSTANT)................Paris

Born at Rennes. Pupil of Lecompte and Vernet. Medals, 1875, 1880. Legion of Honor, 1878.

BOGERT (GEORGE H.).

BLACKMAN (WALTER).............................London

Born at Chicago. Pupil of Gérôme.

BONHEUR (MARIE ROSA) ....Paris

Born at Bordeaux, March 22, 1822. Pupil of her father, Raymond Bonheur. Began by copying in the Louvre; afterward made studies and sketches near Paris. Her first two pictures, exhibited at Bordeaux, 1841, attracted much attention, and were followed by others which established her world-wide fame. During the Franco-Prussian war, her studio and residence were respected by special order of the Crown Prince of Prussia. Since 1849 she has been Director of the Paris Free School of Design for Young Girls, which she founded. Elected member of Antwerp Institute in 1868. Medals, 1845, 1848, 1865, 1867 (*Exposition Universelle*). Cross of the Legion of Honor, 1865. Cross of the Order of Leopold, 1880. Commander's Cross of the Royal Order of Isabella the Catholic, 1880. Conceded to be

the greatest female painter the world has produced. Her celebrated " Horse Fair," in the Stewart collection, was sold for
$53,000, and now hangs in the Metropolitan Museum.

BRILLOUIN (Louis Georges)........................Paris

Born at Saint-Jean-d'Angély. Pupil of Drölling and of Cabat.
Medals, 1865, 1869, and 1874.

CASANOVA-Y-ESTORACH (Antonio)..............Paris

Born at Tortosa, Spain, August 9, 1847. Pupil of Lorenzale
and of Madrazo.

CAZIN (Jean Charles)...............................Paris

Born at Samer (Pas-de-Calais), France. Pupil of Lecoq de
Boisbaudran. Medal, first class, 1880. Legion of Honor,
1882.

COL (David).....................................,Antwerp

Born at Antwerp, 1822. Pupil of De Keyser and Antwerp
Academy. Medal, Vienna Exposition, 1873. Chevalier of the
Order of Leopold, 1875.

COROT (JEAN-BAPTISTE-CAMILLE), dec'd.

Born in Paris, 1796. Was first instructed by Michallon, afterward by Victor Bertin, then spent several years in Italy. Medals, Paris, 1838, 1848, 1855, 1867 (*Exposition Universelle*). Chevalier of the Legion of Honor, 1846. Officer of the same, 1867. Died, 1875. Diploma to the Memory of Deceased Artists (*Exposition Universelle*), 1878.

DAUBIGNY (CHARLES FRANÇOIS), dec'd.

Born in Paris, 1817. Pupil of his father and Paul Delaroche, and for three years studied in Italy. Medals, 1848, 1853, 1855, 1857, 1859, 1867. Chevalier of the Legion of Honor, 1859. Officer of the same, 1874. Died, 1878. Diploma to the Memory of Deceased Artists (*Exposition Universelle*), 1878.

DECAMPS (ALEXANDRE GABRIEL), dec'd.

Born in Paris, 1803. Died, 1860. Pupil of Abel de Pujol, David, and Ingres. Travelled in the East in 1827, after which he devoted himself to painting Oriental subjects. Medals, 1831, 1834. Chevalier of the Legion of Honor, 1839. Officer of the same, 1851.

DE NEUVILLE (ALPHONSE MARIE), dec'd

Born at Saint Omer, France, 1836. A member of a wealthy family, his parents intended him for an official career, but he was only willing to join the army and entered the school at Lorient. Here his astonishing skill in drawing was remarked. In order to make peace with his family he went to Paris and entered the law school, but he spent more time at the military school and in the Champs-de-Mars, sketching and becoming familiar with all the details of a soldier's life. He returned home declaring he would be a painter or nothing. His friends endeavored to discourage his determination, and the artists upon whom he called in Paris advised him to go back home. Delacroix. however, became his friend, and with him De Neuville spent many hours. He studied also with Picot. De Neuville's first pictures were not particularly remarkable, but the Franco-Prussian war gave him inspiration and subjects almost without limit, and since that time the artist has produced some of the greatest battle-pictures of any time. Medals, Paris, 1859, 1861. Chevalier of the Legion of Honor, 1873. Officer of the same, 1881. Died, 1885.

DIAZ DE LA PENA (NARCISSE VIRGILE), dec'd.

Born in Bordeaux, 1809, of parents who had been banished from Spain on account of political troubles. At ten years of age Diaz was left an orphan, and at fifteen he was apprenticed to a maker of porcelain, where his talent first displayed itself. He quarrelled with and left his master, and subsequently spent several years in most bitter poverty. After his ability as a most wonderful colorist had been recognized, Diaz painted and sold many pictures, endeavoring, by the accumulation of a fortune, to avenge the poverty of his youth. He died in 1876. Medals in 1844, 1846, 1848. Chevalier of the Legion of Honor,

1851. Diploma to the memory of Deceased Artists (*Exposition Universelle*), 1878.

DUPRÉ (JULES), dec'd.

Born at Nantes, 1812. When a boy he studied design in the porcelain manufactory of his father, but soon turned his attention to landscape painting, and made his *début* at the Salon, 1831. Medal, 1833. Chevalier of the Legion of Honor, 1849. Medal (*Exposition Universelle*), 1867. Officer of the Legion of Honor, 1870. Died, 1889.

FORTUNY-Y-CARBO (MARIANO), dec'd.

Born at Rëus, in Catalonia, 1838. Died in Rome, 1874. Pupil of Palau, of Lorenzalez, and of the Barcelona Academy, where he won the Prix de Rome in 1856. At Rome, which thenceforth became his residence, he studied Raphael and made sketches of Roman life. In 1859 he was sent to Morocco by the Government to paint the incidents of General Prim's campaign. In 1866 he went to Paris, and then to Madrid, where he remained three years studying the works of Velasquez, Ribera, and Goya. His original style, correct drawing, and

fine color gained for him a great reputation, and the sale of the
contents of his studio after his death brought 800,000 francs.

FRÈRE (PIERRE ÉDOUARD), dec'd.

Born at Paris, 1819. Pupil of Paul Delaroche. Medals at
Paris, 1850, 1852, 1855. Chevalier of the Legion of Honor,
1855. Died, 1886.

HAGBORG (AUGUST)..................................Paris

Born at Gothenburg, Sweden. Pupil of Stockholm Academy,
and in Paris of Palmaroli. Medal, 1879.

HOBBEMA (MEYNDERT), dec'd.

Born at Koeverden or at Amsterdam, 1638. Died at Amsterdam, 1709. Landscape painter. Educated himself under the
influence of Jacob van Ruysdael. Much neglected in his time,
and little esteemed, he now takes rank as one of the greatest
masters of landscape art. He excels in atmospheric effects, in
tone, and in brilliancy of color.

JACQUE (CHARLES ÉMILE)............................Paris

> Born at Paris, 1813. Early in life studied with a geographical engraver. Later, spent seven years in the army, and worked two years in England as an engraver on wood. Is famous for his etchings as well as his paintings. Medals, Paris, 1861, 1863, 1864, 1867. Chevalier of the Legion of Honor, 1867.

JOHNSON (DAVID), N.A........................New York

> Born in New York, 1827. Elected member of the National Academy, New York, 1862. Medal, Philadelphia, 1876. One of the founders of the Artists' Fund Society.

KOWALSKI (VON WIERUSZ ALFRED)...................Paris

> Born in Warsaw, Poland. Pupil of Brandt. Medal, 1878, 1883.

LAMBINET (ÉMILE), dec'd.

> Born at Versailles, 1810. Pupil of Drölling. Medals, Paris, 1843, 1853, 1857. Chevalier of the Legion of Honor, 1867. Died, 1878.

MÉDARD (Eugène) . . . . Paris

Born at Paris. Pupil of Cogniet and of Gérôme. Medals, 1879, 1886.

MEISSONIER (Jean Louis Ernest) . . . . Paris

Born at Lyons, 1813. He went to Paris when quite young, and was for a time a pupil of Léon Cogniet. First exhibited at the Salon in 1836. His picture, "The Brawl" (1855), was purchased by Napoleon III. and presented to the late Prince Albert of England. Medals, Paris, 1840, 1841, 1843, 1848. Grand Medal of Honor, 1855 (*Exposition Universelle*). One of the eight Grand Medals of Honor (*Exposition Universelle*), 1867; Grand Medal of Honor (*Exposition Universelle*), 1878. Chevalier of the Legion of Honor, 1846; Officer of the same, 1856; Commander of the same, 1867; Grand Officer of the same, 1878. Member of the Institute of France, 1861. Honorary member of the Royal Academy, London.

MICHEL (Georges), dec'd.

Born, 1763. Died, 1843.

MILLET (Jean François), dec'd.

Born at Greville, France, 1814. Pupil of Langlois at Cherbourg. The Municipality of Cherbourg gave him a small pension that he might go to study in Paris. Became pupil of Paul Delaroche in 1837, and the friend of Corot, Rousseau, Dupré, and Diaz. Medals, Paris, 1853, 1864, 1867 (*Exposition Universelle*). Chevalier of the Legion of Honor, 1868. Died, 1875. Diploma to the Memory of Deceased Artists, 1878.

MILLET (François).................................. Paris

Son and pupil of his father, Jean François Millet, deceased.

PORTELJE (Gérard)..............................Antwerp

RICHET (Léon).......................................Paris

Born at Solesmes. Pupil of Diaz, Lefebvre, and Boulanger. Honorable mention, Salon, Paris, 1885.

ROUSSEAU (P. E. THÉODORE), dec'd.

Born at Paris, 1812. Pupil of Lethiere. Showed himself a naturalist from the first, and for thirteen years was excluded from the Salon by an Academic jury. First exhibited in 1833. Medals, 1834, 1849, 1855. Chevalier of the Legion of Honor, 1852. One of the eight Grand Medals of Honor (*Exposition Universelle*), Paris, 1867. Died, 1867. Diploma to the Memory of Deceased Artists, 1878.

SAVINI (A.)...................................Rome

STAMMEL (PROF. EBERHARD)....................Dusseldorf

Born in Duren, 1832. Studied at Dusseldorf under Sohn, also at Antwerp, Paris, and Munich.

TAMBURINI (ANTONIO).............................Rome

TROYON (CONSTANTINE), dec'd.

Born at Sevres, 1810. Died, 1865. Pupil of Rivereux. Medals, 1838, 1840, 1848, 1855. Chevalier of the Legion of Honor, 1849. Member of the Academy of Amsterdam. Diploma to the Memory of Deceased Artists, 1878.

CATALOGUE.

₊ DIMENSIONS ARE GIVEN IN INCHES, AND REFER TO CANVAS OR PANEL, EXCLUSIVE OF FRAME. THE FIRST FIGURES INDICATE THE HEIGHT, THE SECOND THE WIDTH.

No. 1

LOUIS-GEORGES BRILLOUIN

"Memories"

10¾ x 8½

8v

Immersed in reflection, an old gentleman, whose social condition is indicated by the sober richness of his attire, sits upon a stone bench, in a park green with the ripeness of midsummer. It is easy to discover in his pensive attitude, with his hands resting on the head of his staff, a dreamer, who, in the (to the spectator) unseen pageant passing before him in this familiar place, holds a phantom review of the past. Around him is the vitality of nature and the vivaciousness of life. He and his thoughts have passed the boundary line of vigorous existence, and he lives his appointed time out in communion with his memories. The red suit of the figure and the green background constitute a perfect harmony of color made brilliant by intrinsic strength instead of artificial contrast.

A pleasant little story, not without a touch of pathos, attaches to this picture. While the painter was still a student under Drölling, with no special idea as to his future steps in art, he frequently encountered in his rambles in the Bois de Boulogne an old gentleman, quaintly attired in the fashion of a previous generation, who always sat upon the same seat, motionless, thoughtful, evidently dozing his long life away heedless of the hurrying world and its cares. He was the last member of a noble family, impoverished by the Revolution, but pensioned by some old family friend more fortunate in worldly gear than he. Years after the old gentleman of the Bois had passed beyond the necessity of pensions, and when the young art student had become a famous artist, chance sent him a model who reminded him of his old acquaintance of the park, and with picturesque liberties of costume Brillouin painted him as he is here.

No. 2

A. SAVINI

"The Web of Fate"

10 x 13

The web of fate has often been spun for man in such fashion as this. The whir of the spinning-wheel has swelled and slackened in rhythmic harmony with the tinkle of the mandolin and the soft pleadings of the idle cavalier who has come to terminate his courtship for good or ill. Summer sunlight blazes in the chateau garden. The harmony of nature, through the open casement, has accompanied those evoked by love and labor within. And now the decisive moment has arrived. The lute is laid aside. The wheel has buzzed itself to rest. That the web woven by fate and made fast by Cupid will be rudely broken, no suggestion of the picture gives us any authority for believing.

Savini is best known as a painter of episodes of this character, trifling in themselves, but made agreeable by their charm of color, their sparkling execution, and the suggestiveness with which their stories are told. Life and love are quite as romantic to-day as they were three centuries ago; but in the past they enjoyed the advantage of surroundings which added picturesqueness to sentiment and lent them an attractiveness to the eye quite independent of their appeal to the intelligence. That they should appeal to the artistic mind as strongly as they do is but natural, and that they should strike a responsive chord in the popular heart is equally comprehensible and just.

No. 3

J. B. C. COROT

"A Mediæval Ruin"

9 × 11

Through a vista of the forest, framed in with great trees, one sees, beyond the precipitous verge of the foreground, a savage and wooded ravine, out of which rises a tempest-scarred crag, crowned by a mediæval ruin. It is a last decaying souvenir of the days when the robber barons levied taxes on all who passed their castles, perched upon almost inaccessible summits above the common highway, both for purpose of defence and of observation of the approach of prey. Corot's subject for this sketch was found on one of the old roads in the south of France by which traffic and travel passed into Italy; and the castle, the abode of the owl and the adder when the artist fixed its passing existence with his brush, had been, according to local legend, the stronghold in the past of one of the most formidable bands of robbers in old Provence.

Corot, the son of thrifty bourgeois parents, was, upon leaving school, sent by his father to serve his apprenticeship with a cloth merchant. He proved a recalcitrant pupil of the trade, given to sketching landscapes on the bill-heads and adorning the business correspondence of the house with original designs. His master gave him up in despair. "He is no good in the shop," said he, "perhaps he may be worth his salt out of doors." So young Corot was sent out with samples of cloth and trimmings to drum up trade among the small retailers and little tailors of Paris. He was given all the out of fashion and unsalable odds and ends in the shop, and his failure to find a market for them led to his dismissal. The elder Corot raved and stormed, but his son had fixed his resolution to become a painter, and could not be moved by threats or persuasions to another Essay at the pleasures of commercial life. After a long contest his father, who was well-to-do and quite able to afford him the indulgence, consented to gratify his ambition, and Corot was entered at the studio of Victor Bertin as a pupil. "And so," he was wont to say, "from handling cloths that would not sell, I took to manufacturing cloths for which I soon found that there was even less of a market. But there was, at any rate, the pleasure of creation and production here, whether it sold or not."

2

No. 4

JULES DUPRÉ

"The Willow Brook"

8½ x 10½

A little river flows serenely between banks of greensward and
harvest fields, and palisades of old oaks and dwarf willows. On
the mirror-like surface of the stream, the color of the sky, which
has a centre of illuminated cloud, is reflected. The coloring is in
the artist's ripest richness, and the little canvas has the power of the
most spacious work. Dupré was excessively fond of these cabinet
pieces, because he believed that he could in them illustrate his
theory, that mere size had nothing to do with the aspect of a
picture ; that the immensity of nature could be rendered quite as
well in the space of inches as in that of yards.

Of Jules Dupré, Mr. Theodore Child wrote from Paris, to *The Sun* of this
city, on the occasion of his death last October, an admirable study, of which
the following is a part :

" Born at Nantes in 1811, son of a porcelain manufacturer, he was taught
industrial drawing at an early age, but having shown a taste for painting he
was sent to Paris and studied in the atelier of M. Diébold. He first exhibited
at the Salon of 1831, and then travelled all over France and England sketching
and making pictures. In 1833 he obtained a second-class medal at the Salon ;
at the Universal Exhibition of 1867, another second-class medal ; in 1849 he was
created Knight of the Legion of Honor ; in 1870 he was promoted officer ;
at the Exhibition of 1889 he obtained a medal of honor, and his name was on
the list for promotion to the grade of Commander of the Legion of Honor.
Dupré was the last of the men of that generation full of flame and fury, of
excess of strength and splendid exaggeration, which revolutionized artistic
France after the historical days of July, 1830. His pictures dazzle eyes that
are accustomed to sober gray ; but as Gautier has said : ' These violent men,
whose very name made the Institute shudder with horror, were gloriously in
the right. Do what he will, man is always below the ideal and the real, and
his most superlative effort, far from going beyond the mark, scarcely even
reaches it.' "

190

No. 5

A. TAMBURINI

"The Pride of the Cellar"

12½ x 10

An old convent cellarer has been sent to procure the prize wine of his bins for the enjoyment of some monkish revellers. He clasps the great wicker-covered flask in his arms as a father might carry his sleeping child. His eyes dwell on it with regret at parting, tempered by a longing for a sip of its time-ripened contents and a sniff at their bouquet. Over the years during which it has lain at *250* rest his memory travels back as he bears it to the sacrifice. It has, perhaps, outlived all the hands that plucked its grapes and pressed their life-blood out to be sealed up in a dusky vault until the alchemy of nature should make every drop within the dust-buried bottle as precious as pure gold. But its day of doom has sounded at last. In a few hours more, there will be nothing left of it but a shattered flask upon the rubbish heap, and the recollection of the cellarer who guarded it so long.

A native of Florence, and the holder of medals of honor at the Exhibitions of Florence and of Rome, Antonio Tamburini possesses also, among collectors, a popularity which is easily his due. His pictures are characterized by purity and clearness of color, a modest brilliancy of effect, and a painstaking but not laborious technique. His monkish subjects are esteemed his best. The Italian spirit of good-humored satire of the ecclesiastical institutions, to which the country nevertheless bows humbly, is strong within him. He has his jest at the expense of the Church, and yet is a devout son to it, and the Church laughs at the joke upon itself, and grants the jester ready absolution for his effervescent irreverence.

1440

No. 6

CARLETON WIGGINS

"In the Orchard"

12 x 18

The scene is a Long Island orchard, within the confines of the historic Hamptons. Under the hardy fruit-trees, gnarled and twisted by the winds that sweep in from the sea, sheep are grazing on the short but juicy turf. Beyond the orchard fence, basking in sunlight, are grainfields and stacks of hay. The season of the summer is drawing to its end, and field and orchard are ripe for the hand of the harvester.

The eastern end of Long Island, once famous from its association with the Beecher family, has become to-day an artistic colony which holds in a proportionate relation to New York the place that Barbizon does with Paris. A few years ago its discovery as a sketching ground was hailed with delight by the little coterie of painters who constituted the famous Tile Club. After they had explored the ground and pointed the way, others of the guild followed in their footsteps. At first it was merely sketching parties that invaded the Hamptons, spending a few weeks of the summer there, but after a time an actual artistic settlement began. Artists, weary of the country boarding-house, built summer cottages and studios for themselves, or transformed the ancient habitations of the district to suit their needs. Easthampton became their special abiding-place. The availability of the district to the city, from which it is but a few hours removed by rail, and the fact that it offered subjects equally to the landscape and figure painter, to the painter of cattle and the painter of the sea, attracted to it representatives of every walk in native art, among the first of whom was Mr. Wiggins, who has found some of his most attractive subjects among its old orchards and its breezy downs.

No. 7

GEORGE H. BOGERT

1640

"The Seine at Ivry"

14 × 20

The river is busy with barges, the freight-carriers of the Seine, which travel to and from the factories and their metropolitan markets of supply or sale. The shore is busy with the factories themselves, with chimneys belching smoke, and all the stir of industry at full speed. One could scarcely expect to find a less favorable subject for artistic treatment than the hard, mechanical aspect and employment of a manufacturing suburb of a great city ; but what with the brightness and sparkle of river and sky, and the varied outlines and masses of the workshops and other structures which make up the composition, the artist has produced a picture whose technical treatment invites commendation, while in its entirety it appeals with pleasing effect to the eye.

105

Forty miles from Paris is Ivry-la-Bataille, where Henry IV. administered such a drubbing to the Duke de Mayenne, as Macaulay commemorates it in his stirring ballad. It is a place of history alone : one of the dullest and sleepiest towns in France, forgotten by most people in its rural desuetude. Ivry-sur-Seine, however, is quite a different community. It is one of the most busy and thriving of industrial cities. It is a suburb of Paris, which has become a centre for the manufacture of glass, earthenware, and chemicals, and forms part of the circle of fortifications built for the defence of the city ; the fort of Ivry, on the left bank of the Seine, being one of the most powerful in the girdle of protectors of the gay city. The river above Paris has, thanks to its atmospheric advantages, the alternating variety of its rural and suburban scenery and its accessibility to the city, long been a favorite sketching route for the artist, who, as Mr. Bogert shows us, finds even in unromantic, practical, and industrious Ivry itself, material plastic to his brush. The placid river, scarcely ruffled by a ripple, the clear, cool sky, which, once you get away from the smoke fog of Paris, has the tint of opal and of pearl. the barges, picturesque in their slow-moving ungainliness, modify the ugliness of the shore, and lend their picturesqueness of form and color to the redemption of the scene.

1745

No. 8

C. STAMMEL

"A Pleasing Discovery"

15½ x 13

There has been a great deal of negotiating over this bond before it was carried to the point which made the affixing of the great leaden seal a concluding operation of the contract. Under such circumstances, the terms and clauses of the compact should certainly have been defined without mistakes. But for all that, the thrifty old money-lender, whose strong-boxes have disgorged some of their store to further a spendthrift on his brief career, has discovered a flaw in them which adds cent-per-cent to his interest, and lights his shrewd old face up with a smile which he is too politic to allow to become a grin of satisfaction, even in the privacy of his own sanctum.

A painter of many episodes of this character, in which the suggestion of the story is never spoiled by a coarse effort at direct·effect, Stammel, among all the artists of Dusseldorf to-day, probably ranks highest in his power of utilizing the simple facts of nature for the best results. His natural predilection is for the study of textures, and for experiments in rich color applied in simple schemes, which renders this choice of subjects particularly agreeable to him, and makes his treatment of them happiest. The face of the money-lender is said to be a portrait, very vividly limned from memory, of one of the most opulent and widest known usurers in Germany.

No. 9

ALFRED KOWALSKI
"Belated"

R. G. Dun

1900

8½ x 8½

The day is late, and the night wind is rising bitter with frost. It is almost the hour for the gray wolf to slink from its hungry ambush in the snow-mantled thicket, and the huntsman has yet a smart ride between himself and shelter and supper, not to mention safety. A weary steed cannot stop to count its footsteps, when urged by the fury of impatience not unmingled with anxiety. Already the wayfarer can see dark spots that move along the horizon with a sinister significance to him, and the snowy steppe is measured with long bounds as the spurred and flogged jade bears its master forward in his frantic race against the night and its terrors.

350

The life of the Polish people, which still preserves so much of its patriarchal picturesqueness, has furnished material for a little body of modern painters in Munich and in Paris, generally Poles themselves, which has produced much spirited and brilliant work. Of the group of Poles educated at the Munich Art Schools, Alfred Kowalski is probably the most noteworthy. Friederich Pecht, the great German critic, speaks of him as a remarkable talent, and especially commends his frequent touches of humor, and the fine national character that he secures in his pictures. Kowalski is a huntsman and a wild horseman, as well as a painter, and his subjects are rendered invariably from personal observation. One snowy night he rode up to a posting-house on the Polish steppes, his horse exhausted and himself shaking with excitement. He had been chased some miles by wolves. He greeted the party of Russian officers of his acquaintance, who were gathered at supper, with a shout, " Such a subject ! But upon my honor I was afraid at one time I should not live to paint it." The picture was exhibited by him the following year, and is now in the Russian imperial collection.

1250

No. 10

DAVID JOHNSON, N.A.

"The River Road"

12 X 16

The land has been refreshed by a summer shower, and the sunset makes a play of brilliant color amid the rifted clouds still heavy with moisture. Gathering shades of evening additionally enrich a landscape ripe with the full fruition of the year. The waters of a placid and shallow little river reflect the sombre shadows of a clump of trees in the middle distance, and the country stretches away beyond, to the horizon, with a last gleam of light marking its undulations. The river road is tracked out upon the grassy bank in the foreground, and at the margin of the stream two seated figures are seen. True and powerful in color and admirable in composition, the picture represents the painter in the plenitude of his power.

Born in New York in 1827, David Johnson's art is a product entirely of personal study and observation. Although he received a few preliminary lessons from Jasper F. Cropsey, the painter really found in Nature his true teacher and master. He has, of all the great American landscape painters, acquired least by contact with the art of Europe, and his style is essentially the result of experiment and individual intelligence and feeling. He has never been abroad, and his works all illustrate, with a remarkably level, high standard of excellence, types of familiar native scenery. A fine harmony of rich color is one of their distinguishing characteristics. With this is allied a massive dignity of composition and a firm and accurate rendition of form. These qualities have won for the artist a place in American art similar to that of Rousseau in France.

No. 11

NARCISSE DIAZ DE LA PEÑA

"The Forest's Depth"

8½ x 11

The mystery of the wildwood ever possessed for Diaz a subtle charm. It was not only for what he saw in it, but for what it hid, that he loved to paint it. He dwelt upon such subjects with a lingering adoration, and wherever he is seen at his best it is in one of these shadowy scenes, full of lurking splendors of rich color, accentuated by flashes of light from casual breaks in the vault of verdure, with openings in which glimmer the waters of a forest pool, where the deer may drink and the blackcock bathe, secure from the murderous interruption of an intruding human foot. The artist, armed with his brush, has privileges in such a spot which the hunter, equipped for slaughter, never can enjoy.

A magnificent individuality in the personnel of art is that of the wooden-legged painter of the Forest of Fontainebleau, sturdy and indomitable combatant, proud and disdainful of the favors of life, who won his artistic victory by the undeviating force of his personal confidence. He begged no man to buy of him. When picture dealers and collectors alike shrugged their shoulders at his canvases he said, " Very well, I can afford to keep' them," and so stumped off to starve, like a soldier in the field, who, when his rations are short, buckles his belt a hole tighter and looks to the enemy for his next meal. Of all the painters of the Barbizon group, Diaz was the most distinguished personally, because the man had in him embers of the fiery Spanish spirit that makes proud poverty a virtue and genius a sacred thing. In life as in art, he was ever a master, a magister, and above all a man.

No. 12

GEORGES MICHEL

"Harvesters of the Sea"

13 X 17

The sea is darkened by the shadow of a stormy sky, in which the
light of calm still struggles for supremacy. The fishermen, harvest-
ers of the sea, who reap a scanty subsistence at a measureless price
of peril and of toil, have made for land under the threat of the
tempest to come. Some have already beached their boats. Others
are scudding shoreward before the puffing gale. On a rocky head-
land in the middle plane, the sturdy ruin of an old castle, mantled
in ivy. provides a beacon for them to steer by into safety. As in all
of Michel's best pictures, the contrast between the turbulency of the
blustrous sky and the sombre solidity of the earth is made strikingly
effective.

Georges Michel, born in Paris on January 12, 1763, was one of the most
extraordinary characters in the history of art in France. He was a sturdy
little man, witty and vain, and naturally gifted as an artist. He painted for
pure love of painting, disdained all schools and traditions in art, and produced
an incredible number of pictures, to which he never signed his name unless
requested by a purchaser to do so ; because, as he put it, "No man will ever
paint like me ; consequently my pictures require no signature." Michel was
the real founder of the school of naturalism of which Millet, Rousseau, Dias,
Corot, and their contemporaries are the accepted apostles. He died on June
7, 1843.

No. 13

3 3 5̄0

LOUIS GEORGE BRILLOUIN

"The Bookworm"

14 × 11

A prim and precise old gentleman, whose scrupulous neatness of attire makes his grimy surroundings doubly dingy by contrast, has meandered into the shop of a junkman, seduced by the prospect of a prize among the battered volumes heaped up in a corner. He has 2 / 0 found a book to his taste ; and, lost to everything but it, he devours it page by page, undisturbed by the chaffering of sordid trade and the squalid atmosphere about him. Meanwhile, the proprietor of the shop, secure of the customer who has quartered himself upon him, leaves him to himself, and dickers in the doorway with a peasant, who is looking for a bargain in old iron, or a set of second-hand shoes for his bony team.

The circumstances under which Brillouin chanced upon the subject for this characteristic picture form a little historiette in themselves. During one of his summer vacations, he found himself in one of the border cities of France— possibly in Strasbourg. The landlord of his hotel became interested upon the discovery that his guest was a painter, and exhibited to him several authentic and valuable antiquities that he treasured among his household gods. These he said he had obtained from a certain second-hand dealer near by, who sold every- thing, from pictures and books down to worn-out sabots and broken crockery. Brillouin, interested in turn, sought out this magazine of illimitable possibili- ties, and secured from his exploration of it a number of objects of quaint antiquity which he added to the treasures of his studio. Beyond this he secured the close and faithful study of the shop itself, which served him for a back- ground for his figure of the bookworm, and formed the groundwork of one of his most successful pictures.

3 5 60

No. 14

CHARLES ÉMILE JACQUE

"Porte de Bergerie"

13 x 9½

The blue-bloused shepherd is calling his flock out of the fold.
The leaders advance hesitatingly, pushed by others behind them, into
the bright daylight from which they have been shut up. The end of
an inclement season has arrived, and the flock is destined for one of
the long pasturages, as the shepherd's haversack, loaded with black-
bread and strong cheese for his own nourishment, shows.

Charles Jacque is the most variously gifted artist of his nation and time in
the diversity of his technique. He commenced active life at the age of seven-
teen as an engraver of maps. When he tired of this, which was very soon, he
enlisted as a soldier. After seven years of service in the ranks he went back
to map engraving, but only for a brief space. While in the army he had cultivated his natural talent for drawing, and one morning he resigned his topo-
graphical work forever and went in quest of a job as a draughtsman on wood.
He found one, and shortly after emigrated to England, where he obtained
regular employment, both in making original drawings on the block and in
copying paintings for engraving on wood. He had already begun experi-
menting as an etcher, and to him may be ascribed the origin of the great
modern revival in the art. He painted also, generally rustic scenes. His first
successes in oil were made with pictures of poultry, for which he had such a
passion that he bred cocks and hens in his bedroom at his lodgings. These
were at once his pets and his models. As soon as Jacque found that his etch-
ings were popular enough to pay for publication he devoted himself largely to
their production. Their aggregate is estimated at over 500 plates, forming a
number of valuable series of rustic scenes. He contributed also striking caricatures to *Charivari*, experimented in lithography, and painted in water
colors and pastel. To everything be brought an individual touch and spirit.
The popularity of his paintings was not long in enabling him to abandon his
hack work for the wood engravers, to which he never returned. He has produced little of recent years, living in retirement on his farm, of which it is said
the chicken houses occupy more space than does the artist's home.

No. 15

GERARD PORTELJE

" The Old Campaigner "

18 x 24

3930

A veteran of the great wars, wounded and laid aside from the ranks, is on his homeward way, to a future of superfluous old age, the long familiar musket replaced by a pacific bundle and stick. He has halted at a wayside tavern, where over his modest refreshment he entertains the *garde champêtre*, the landlord, and one of the cronies of the peaceful house with some of the thrilling stories of his campaigns, that no doubt lose none of their romance in the recital. The rustics listen, absorbed in interest and admiration, and, thanks to the old soldier's eloquence, almost imagine themselves actors in the stirring scenes he describes. Executed in the painter's best style and spirit.

305

Among a certain class of subject painters, Portelje has long held high popular rank. He possesses in an eminent degree the faculty of the story-teller, while his technical ability is of a high order. There may be scored to his credit a number of admirably executed canvases, which, entirely apart from their value as compositions with a narrative purpose, possess a merit of their own for accuracy of drawing, discriminating skill in color, and an execution at once frank and complete. The tavern interior shown in this picture is a study of a historical wayside hostelry, whose association with the incidents of the later Napoleonic campaigns no doubt suggested to the artist the subject for the little page from the book of real life for which he made it the frame.

4235

No. 16

EDWIN LORD WEEKS

"The Pottery Merchant"

25½ x 20

The entire stock in trade of a Hindoo pottery merchant is exposed for sale in front of his shop. There are all varieties of native earthenware, from the great porous water-jars and the double-armed goglets, in which water is cooled, down to rice dishes and a bit or two of glazed ware, poor enough in itself, but fine by contrast with its humble associates in trade. The painter has given careful attention to the different textures and qualities of clay of which these objects are composed, with successful results. The pottery merchant himself, sheltered in his dark little cabin from the sunlight that blazes on the outer walls and on the roof overgrown with vegetation, bargains with a customer in the doorway, whose yellow robe provides the keynote for the color of the picture.

While Egypt and North Africa have long been popular subject sources, especially for the painters of France and Spain, but few of the artists of our day have ventured into the remoter Orient in search of material for their brushes. Perhaps the most noteworthy of these exceptional adventurers is Mr. Weeks. Like the others he began his voyages with trips from the studios of Bonnat and Gérôme to Cairo, and sojourns in Moorish Spain, in Morocco, Tangiers, and Algiers. Thence he drifted to Jerusalem and Damascus, and finally, looking still farther afield, to India. His pictures from this latter field are those which have attracted most attention of late years. The novelty of the life they depict, its garish splendor of color and barbaric sumptuousness of adornment and ceremonial, familiar as they have been made by printed descriptions, are presented by the painter with a vividness doubly forcible and striking, dressed as they are in a commensurate dazzle of sunlight, and a power of glowing and gleaming color in nature, that offsets that in the humanity which animates it.

4445

No. 17

WALTER BLACKMAN

"An American Girl"

18½ x 15

Mr. Blackman has presented us with a more charming type of an American girl than once did Mr. Henry James. He shows her to us in profile, with a roseate background, her fair face rather pensive in expression, and her downcast eyes softened by the tenderness of dreams. The picture is an idealized portrait of the highest type, in which every detail, from the splendid crown of chestnut hair to the filmy drapery that veils the shapely shoulders, is rendered by the artist with a delicately sensitive hand.

185

Of all the pupils of Gérôme whom America can claim as native to her soil, Mr. Blackman betrays, perhaps, the least subjection to the methods of his master. His talent, without being largely ambitious, has a decidedly original bent, and while one occasionally finds suggestions of the Gérôme school in his smooth and polished *technique*, no traces of mere imitation are discoverable in him. The artist is especially happy in rendering the more delicate types of female beauty, to which he always lends an ideal quality that removes them from the realm of portraiture into that of creative art.

4630

4630

No. 18

LÉON RICHET

"The Border of the Forest"

15 x 18

230

A scene on the outskirts of the forest of Fontainebleau, which
one might almost imagine from the brush of Diaz. It is, in fact,
the production of a pupil who adopted much of his master's style.
A group of trees occupies the foreground. Beyond one sees an
open landscape, lighted through the middle distance from a clouded
sky. The coloring is rich and strong, and the picture harmonious
in tone and solid in quality.

The works are but little known in America of this devoted pupil of a great
artist, who has himself reached a degree of unqualified eminence in his art.
The charming pictures of Richet command an appreciation from French
collectors and connoisseurs that prevents their finding their way into an open
market, except by the accident of the disposal of a collection. The greater
number of his subjects are found at Fontainebleau, where he paints over the
ground that Diaz cultivated to such artistic effect, and this fact adds not a
little to the suggestion of that master that the pictures of his pupil convey.
Richet has been an *exempt* of the Salon since 1885, and in 1888 received a third
class medal.

4860

4860

No. 19

JEAN BAPTISTE CAMILLE COROT

" The Bridge "

J. Wolfe

11 x 16½

' In Corot's pictures, studies, and sketches, one may read the history of his travels. This is a page from his roamings in Southern Europe. A vast landscape, rocky and bare, extends in broken planes and irregular masses, under the ardent blue sky of the South. From an elevation in the foreground, over which a road passes, we look down upon the windings of a river which the road crosses by an ancient, castellated bridge, evidently built to dominate the highway as well as further its progress over the stream. Solitude adds gravity to the romantic associations of the storied past aroused by the scene.

300

Corot made his first visit to Italy in 1825 and remained there three years. On this and subsequent occasions here, and in the South of France, he secured many subjects of the greatest historical interest for their recording of the decaying and disappearing monuments to early and mediæval civilization : " The Bridge " is one of these. It is a relic of the middle ages, in that portion of the old Roman territories in Gaul, commonly known as Provence. The bridge is said to have long since disappeared, and the river, one of the tributaries of the Rhone, to have become a mere ditch by the silting up under which most of the streams of Southern France have ceased to be navigable.

3

5160

5760

No. 20

JULES DUPRÉ

"A Barbizon Prairie"

9½ x 12½

500

One of the plains on the skirts of the famous forest of Fontainebleau reaches into a distance of purple hills, under a gray and
clouded sky.   The foreground is broken with bushes and irregu-
larities of the richly grassed soil.   In the middle distance are some
oaks, majestic in their superb simplicity of form.   The tone is
subdued, without sombreness.   The color scheme is rich, the effect
powerful, and the execution broad and decided without sacrifice of
completeness in detail or quality.

Dupré's home life at L'Isle Adam, where, separated from his birthplace only
by the width of the river Oise, he lived, worked, and died, was once beauti-
fully described by one of his friends.   "It is," said he, "a modest house,
comfortable with the *bourgeoise* comfort that makes no pretence—a house in
which everything is calculated for the restful pleasure of an industrious life.
No street noise invades its walls to disturb the painter at his labor, which
never ends.   The family, attentive and tender, guard his privacy as a sacred
thing.   Souvenirs of his great friends surround him on the walls—magnificent
drawings by Théodore Rousseau among others, and a superb picture by Corot,
bought by Dupré out of his savings, and which he has refused to part with
even upon an offer of 50,000 francs.   As often happens, a friend is a guest at
the hospitable board, and when the dinner is done, and Dupré has lighted his
pipe, the master talks, and we listen to his souvenirs.   The spirit of his youth
wakes in him again.   His words fill the dim room with glorious phantoms.
The great battle of art wages among the shadows till the pipes are out and the
hour of rest is at hand."

5660

5860

No. 21

THÉODORE ROUSSEAU

"The Walled Farm"

6½ x 12½

1000

An old farm, with rambling outhouses, all surrounded by orchards, is enclosed within a girdle of stout stone walls that give it a mano-rial aspect. Such farms were not uncommon in France half a century ago, and some remain to-day. Over the grassy plain a river flashes in the warm light of late afternoon, and a chain of hills gives variety to the horizon line.

It is said to have been in the vicinity of this farm that the artist obtained the material for his famous masterpiece " Le Givre," or " The Hoarfrost." Monsieur Albert Wolff, in his inimitable " La Capitale de l'Art," recites of this latter great picture, that one morning Jules Dupré entered the apartments of Baroilhet, the then great baritone of the opera, and said : " I have a bargain for you, old boy ; I have a *chef d'œuvre* to sell." " And by whom ? " asked the singer. " Théodore Rousseau." " He certainly has talent," said Baroilhet, " plenty of it ; but money is deuced scarce." " You can pay it in two installments," insinuated Dupré, " 250 francs a month." " And where is your *chef d'œuvre* ? " Dupré signalled from the window, and presently the commissionnaire whom he had left waiting outside entered with his burden. Baroilhet, a man of taste and one of the first to give any encouragement to the painters of 1830, viewed the unveiling of the canvas with enthusiasm. He paid the required sum for the picture, which Dupré had been vainly hawking over Paris all the morning in order to relieve Rousseau's pressing needs, and became the possessor of " Le Givre," which at his sale, twenty years later, commanded the price of 17,000 francs, and which is now numbered among the masterpieces of the Barbizon school in the great private collections of the United States.

6660

No. 22

CONSTANT TROYON

" The Farm "

13 X 11

Troyon, who set out as a landscape painter, was from the start still a diligent student, whenever opportunity offered, of farm life and character. He here gives us, with vigorous and characteristic strokes, full of color and spirit, a corner of an old farmyard, where the poultry forage for food, and some sheep and an old cow gather, as is their gregarious wont, waiting for the familiar call to feed. The character of the scenery, the dwarf willows, and the farm buildings would suggest the scene to be in one of the upper districts of France.

It is said to have been the accident of a trip into Holland that made a cattle painter of Troyon. Previous to that time he had confined himself almost entirely to landscape, and while his productions had been received with the respect their vigor and originality commanded, they had brought him no profitable fame. The fact was, that he was too great a colorist to be able to give full expression to himself in landscape (alone. The pictures of Paul Potter, it is believed, first opened his eyes and gave him a hint as to his true path. After his return to Paris, the public were surprised by the complete transformation in his subjects, and the remarkable advance in their results. His animals, largely painted, with admirable color, fairly lived in landscapes brushed in with a master hand. From this moment, Troyon's success was assured, for the furor for his pictures which then broke out only increased with time, and is even more ardent to-day than when he died.

7320

No. 23

ALEXANDRE GABRIEL DECAMPS

" The Alchemist "

13 × 9¾

The seeker after the philosopher's stone is absorbed in the mystery of his quest in his laboratory. He stands at his furnace, over whose bed of glowing coals some mystic combination which is to transform base metal into gold is being fused. The gravity of his face expresses that of his task. The room, littered with the tools and appliances of his work, is sombre with such shadows as belong to secret employments, prosecuted guardedly behind barred and bolted doors.

158

Without any competent knowledge of the academic rules of art, Decamps was one of the great artists and reformers of his revolutionary time. His work exhibits, in all its phases, the fierce and energetic spirit which swayed its creator, whose childhood was intellectually dwarfed by a parental tyranny which made the boy, with the soul of a poet, the companion of peasants, a little savage of the forests of Picardy, whose power of study was spoiled forever by the freedom of his rude and untrammelled boyhood. Decamps subsequently educated himself, at what cost of self-repression and tireless application only he could have told, but the habits of his robust and unrestricted youth remained with him until the last. One characteristic they developed in him was a love of hunting, and it was while engaged in the chase, in the forest of Fontainebleau, in 1860, that he was thrown from his horse and killed.

7460

7470

No. 24

MARIANO FORTUNY

"A Belle of the Campagna"

6½ x 5½

One of the chief pleasures of the most brilliant period of Fortuny's
life—that which he spent in Rome—was to seek, among the shepherds
and herdsmen of the Campagna, the vanishing types of the great
Latin race, which in its day dominated the civilized world. He
painted some superb examples of these. Here he gives us the head
of an Italian girl, a shepherdess of the Campagna, in the ripeness of
youthful beauty, swarthy, with a mane of black ringleted hair, and a
budding bust that promises a classical symmetry of womanly shapeli-
ness. That he was in love with his subject, the tender touch and
brilliant execution of the picture show.

That Fortuny owed his untimely death to his devotion to his studies in defi-
ance of the treacherous Roman climate, there is no doubt. He had a magnificent
studio in the Eternal City, which he had stuffed with art treasures for which
he traded pictures and sketches with the dealers in antiquities in Italy, Spain,
and Paris. He was in Grenada, painting with an incredible fury of productiveness, when the servant he had left in charge of his Roman studio died.
Fortuny returned to Rome at once, settling there in 1872, never to leave the
city except for a trip to Venice, and in 1873, when the Roman fever prostrated
him, to Portici, where, in a villa by the sea, he was in a fair way to recover his
health, when, encouraged by a slight improvement in his condition, he suddenly
shot off to Rome early in November, 1874. Before the month ended he was
dead. The old fever, aggravated to new power by a cold contracted while
painting out of doors in inclement weather and unhealthy atmosphere, ended
at thirty-five a life which deserved the full limit of man's years of usefulness
to the world. Fortuny died in harness. Upon his death-bed he made a sketch
for Mme. Fortuny's album, of the death-mask of Beethoven, the composer.

No. 25

JEHAN GEORGES VIBERT

8 δ δ δ

"Monsignor at his Ease"

4⅛ x 6¼

Serenely indifferent to the cares of Church and State, his eminence takes his ease in his garden. Stretched at full length on his back, with his head pillowed on his hands, and his eyes shaded by his hat, he lies among the perfumed grasses and the daisies, lulled by the murmur of the willow-shaded brook. His splendid ecclesiastical vestments make a flame of vivid color against the modest verdure, and constitute one of those daring experiments of contrast, of which the artist is so fond. The painter's manifest intention has been to touch with the sly satire which is characteristic of him the luxurious indolence and indifference to worldly cares of a great prince of the Church.

470

Vibert will go down in the history of art as the painter of cardinals, although these form by no means the most numerous class of subjects he has produced. His trenchant satire, and the daring touch with which he handles the magnificence of the cardinals' robes of office, conspire to compel an attention to these pictures, which others, quite as noteworthy perhaps, secure by the gradual process of progressive attractiveness. The sale of "The Missionary's Story," in the Stewart collection, for $25,500, marks the crown of his success in this line. At the sale of the Stebbins collection, in 1889, his "Spanish Diligence Office," a subject of another character, in which he is equally brilliant and masterly, brought $9,100. It is a fact known to comparatively few, that this satirist of the brush is also a keen and witty wielder of the pen. Vibert is passionately fond of the theatre, at which he is an almost nightly attendant, and has contributed notably to its literature. His vaudeville "Le Tribune Mécanique," his comedy "Verglas," and his comic scenes, have won him, in their degree, almost as much commendation as his pictures.

8530

No. 26

CONSTANT TROYON

" Grazing "

7 x 9¾

A black cow with a white face is seen in profile, walking slowly
and grazing as she goes. The lustre of her coat, the ripe and sappy
richness of the grass, the movement of the animal in her sedate
progress over a secure pasturage, are admirably rendered. The
picture is one secured originally from the artist's studio, in which it
was preserved by him as a keynote derived directly from nature and
impossible of duplication.

Among the French artists of his time, Troyon was the greatest traveller. Up
to his death, in 1865, his restless spirit kept him constantly exploring fresh
fields for variations of the subjects to which he had devoted himself. He preserved memoranda of every nook and corner of his own country, and his
works provide also a record of his industrious invasions of Holland, Belgium, and England, which he knew almost as familiarly as France. A tireless
worker, his impatient spirit kept him continually on the rack with the belief
that he was not accomplishing enough. He seldom worked continuously on
one subject, but kept his studio full of pictures in various stages of progress,
which he took up and set aside again as the mood moved him. When his fury
of productiveness reached fever heat, he would depart for relief on one of
those journeys of which "Grazing" is a souvenir.

8820

No. 27

MARIE-ROSA BONHEUR

"Monarch of the Herd"

13 X 20

A splendid Norman bull is dozing in his stall. He is shown in
profile, lying upright, a magnificent bulk of creamy white with
broad black markings, his great shoulders lifted a little, his flanks
relaxed, his hinder leg extended at ease, and his eyes closed. This
study, made under the most favorable auspices from nature, is characterized by subtle beauties of color that are rare in the artist's most
ambitious works. The original was a favorite animal with Mlle.
Bonheur, not only as a model but as a personal pet, reared by her,
and buried when its natural period of life was reached.

1950

Marie-Rosa Bonheur is the daughter of a painter who died in 1853, proud
at having seen his child eclipse his own fame. She was born in Bordeaux in
1822, and at the age of nineteen, in 1841, sent her first pictures to the Salon. She
paints brutes, and she loves the brutes she paints. It is told of her that lions
have been tamed at her gentle touch, and that the regal bulls of the Scotch
Highlands have come to her to have their proud crests scratched. Personally
she is a pure and noble woman, of the largest and most catholic sympathy with
her kind. She was one of, if not the first person in our time to suggest the
establishment of an official system to prevent the shameful cruelty to animals
which her varied studies and investigations into brute life revealed to her.

1077⁰

10770

No. 28

JEAN BAPTISTE CAMILLE COROT

" The Hillside Path "

9½ x 19½

380

To Corot, nature was always grandest in its greatest simplicity. He illustrates it here in a broad and simple study of the crown of a hill, intersected by a narrow path, up which a herdsman ascends toward his flock, which is indicated in the middle plane. Beyond the crest of the hill one obtains a purple glimpse of a distant hill. The sky is radiant and vibrant with the tenderly brilliant light the master loved to paint, the execution is broad and simple, and the composition unostentatiously imposing in its dignified massiveness and the finely felt and suggested contrast of substantial earth and atmospheric immensity of space.

The picture was a favorite with the master, and was purchased from his collection after his death.

It is told of Corot that he was once found painting a study of a blank white wall against a blank blue sky, with just a morsel of creeping vine at one end of the wall, and a few inches of red-tiled roof showing over the other. " You can never make a picture of that," said his friend. " My dear friend," he replied, " It *is* a picture. I hope I may be able to copy it." And in the next Salon, Paris stood breathless before this blazing morsel of the burning South, which is to-day a treasure in one of the great collections of the world. Corot's whole life in art was devoted to the solution of such problems. Light and air he worshipped, as the Parsee the sun, and it is to be recorded of him that his most daring experiments in this direction were commonly his most conspicuous successes.

11150

No. 29.

JULES DUPRÉ

" A Clouded Sky "

11/50

/1 used

The sky is lowering with rain, and shadows the land with a menace of the opening of its floodgates. The mood of the brooding heavens is repeated in the varied inflections of light and shade in the landscape. There is an anticipatory rustle in the leaves of the fine old oak tree in the foreground, and the stream on whose bank it stands reflects in the variations of cool color on its surface the clouds that float above it. In the middle plane a farmhouse and some grazing cattle lend human interest and vitality to the scene. The color is ripe and fresh, with all the harmoniousness of tone and fulness of strength that are a distinguishing characteristic of the artist at his best.

The last survivor of the men of 1830, the revolutionists of French art, died in October, 1889, at the age of seventy-nine. It was to Jules Dupré more than any other that Troyon owed his encouragement and guidance in the earlier years of his artistic self-education, and throughout his life. Dupré was distinguished for the readiness with which he placed himself at the service of his brother artists, with substantial aid as well as mere advice and moral support. Dupré's artistic career was fortunate. The purchase by the Duc de Nemours of the very first picture he exhibited at the Salon made him to a certain extent fashionable, and secured for him a market which other men were many years in obtaining access to. While readily disposing of his own pictures, he was also an active and energetic salesman for those of his friends. In a recent fine obituary article, Mr. Theodore Child sums up his character thus: " Dupré cared for nothing but his art, his family, and his friends. To the end of his life he retained the fever and the enthusiasm of 1830. With his white beard and his long hair he seemed, in his later years, like a venerable apostle. His conversation was grandly poetic, and enamelled with quotations from the great writers. His favorite authors were Montaigne and La Fontaine. Like Jean Jacques Rousseau, who, as Jules Dupré used to say, ' put some green into literature,' this great artist was not content merely to break with the classical and tiresome landscape of the past, nor was he satisfied with simple realism or even with the measured and grave sentiment of his English masters, Constable and Bonington. He might rather be called, so far as inspiration is concerned, a French Turner, but a Turner who had studied assiduously Ruysdael and Hobbema. Jules Dupré's pictures are always full of soul and intense poetry."

No. 30

DAVID COL

11 150

"Suspicion"

12½ x 10

295

An easy-going old bachelor has dined simply but well, as is his wont. In the luxurious lassitude of a replete stomach, he enjoys a waking dream in his arm-chair, while his buxom and comely serving-maid clears the board. She raises the empty wine-bottle to the light, partly suspicious that her master has had a glass too much, and partly to satisfy herself that he has left the flagon burdened with no heeltaps, for whose disappearance she or the cat may be reproached. The background is a comfortable modern Flemish interior. The details, from the salad bowl, the dish of apples, the section of cheese, with its glass cover on the table, to the larger accessories, are treated with the same accuracy of drawing and substantial quality of execution as the figures themselves.

David Col is the master of *genre* painting of modern Belgium. He enjoys an equal reputation for dry wit and a humorously satirical enjoyment of human nature, in real life as in the works in which his mind reflects itself. This picture is an example in point. His popularity, it would appear, has not unnaturally induced unscrupulous men to forgeries of his work. So, on the back of the panel on which "Suspicion" is painted, he has squared off a tablet in white paint, on which he has written in pencil, in bold characters, and before the paint was quite dry, the following quaint pun upon the title and guarantee of the picture's identity combined :

" ' Suspicion.'

" I testify to having painted the picture on the other side : Antwerp, 12 December, 1884. David Col."

11445

11445

No. 31

PIERRE EDOUARD FRÈRE

"Share and Share Alike"

12½ x 9½

260

In a cottage kitchen the little daughter of the house and her good friend, the house-dog, are at luncheon. At least the child is, while her faithful comrade, squatting before her, patiently awaits the moment when he may assert his prerogative of cleaning the bowl. His expression is submissive, but intent. His little mistress gravely encourages him to further exercise of self-denial, for which there will be ample compensation in afternoon romps to come. The surroundings, like the chief objects of the composition, are painted with a simple hand, but scrupulous devotion to the mass of the details; the color is subdued and strong, and the pretty little story is very forcibly told.

Frenchmen regard Pierre Edouard Frère as one of the artistic paradoxes of the century. A full-fledged pupil of Paul Delaroche, the king of classicists in his day, Frère in his productions is one of the leaders of the French realists. He was a modest leader, it is true, both in his subjects and his presentation of their claims upon the public. But the world, which found him out on its own account, has assigned him a permanent place without requesting his permission. Frère has been aptly called the Columbus of country children. He was their discoverer as possible models, and he has given them a rank in art as Millet gave one to the peasant, and Troyon to the ploughman with his oxen and his shaggy dog.

11705

No. 32

ANTONIO CASANOVA Y ESTORACH

11 70⁵

"The Morning Cup"

R. 6. Perkins 7×

580

Father Francisco evidently finds the chocolate to his liking. None but the best could charm such an expansive smile to that contented face. It is the face of one who is competent to decide points of culinary merit, whether they apply to brewing chocolate or baking game pies, and the beverage it beams upon could require no higher praise than its indorsement provides for it. He poises the saucer warily, lest a single fat drop of the rich compound should waste itself upon the barren floor. He absorbs the delicious draught slowly, so that his palate may revel in the repeated luxury of deliberate indulgence, and prolongs the pleasure of the cup by mouthfuls that grow only more savory as they approach their end.

Casanova made his first appearance at the Salon of 1873, being at that time on a business visit to Paris. In 1877 he again figured as an exhibitor, and this time he had come to stay, for he had become a permanent resident of France. The critical and the purely popular voice alike acclaimed the young Spaniard as a worthy addition to the artistic cohort of the capital of art; and the gayety of his moods, no less than the spirit and joyousness of his technique, won him friends and patronage. In 1877, after the critics had accused him of an inclination to trifling and easy rather than serious work, and hinted that he was incapable of grander efforts, Casanova, in the dry, satirical spirit which is part of his nature, prepared a surprise for them that should silence them forever. He sent to the exhibition at the Palais d'Industrie, a huge canvas called "Sword and Gown." The scene was the interior of a convent during the League. The monks were represented, with all the humor and nerve the artist was capable of, arming themselves for the civil war. The figures were life-size, and the treatment masterly. Casanova has not been troubled by the critics since.

12285

285

No. 33

MARIANO FORTUNY

"The Serenade"

15 x 10½

290 An ardent lover has emptied his purse into the lean pouches of a beggar band of Spanish students, in honor of his lady love. They serenade her under her balcony, with the combined harmonies of guitar and mandolin and flute. Their leader twirls his tambourine aloft upon his forefinger, adding the joyous jingle of its metallic castanets to the melodic tribute, over which the provider of the entertainment, draped in his crimson cloak, watches with jealous eyes ; for Spanish señoritas have been known to be fickle before, when beggar students have been comely and bold. For background we have a flash of the lights of the Prado, under the indigo sky of a midsummer night in Madrid.

Fortuny was twenty-eight years of age when he went to Madrid to study and copy after the Spanish old masters. He painted some independent works besides, among them his " Mariposa " and a number of characteristic local episodes, of which " The Serenade " is one. The romantic flavor which still permeates Spanish life and customs, and links the Spain of to-day with the Spain of the days of Cervantes and Velasquez, found an appreciative delineator in the young genius whose original and daring spirit stirred Spanish art out of the sloth and indolence of generations of decadence, into revived life. It was during this first visit to Madrid that Fortuny became the friend of Madrazo, and eventually his son-in-law, and the picture of the serenade may quite warrantably be assumed to be a page out of his own amatory experiences, just as his famous " Spanish Marriage " was suggested by the incidents and ceremonies of his wedding with the Señorita Madrazo.

12575

No. 34

NARCISSE VIRGILE DIAZ (DE LA PEÑA)

"The Forest Pool"

10 X 17

W. J. Hoover

It is a curious fact that, of all the group of painters of which he
made one of the leaders, Diaz, a cripple by the loss of a leg in boyhood, was the one who most thoroughly explored that fertile field of
artistic nature which they have made immortal. He knew all of
their sketching grounds—the willow-shaded rivulets, the plains and
fields and meadows, and the picturesque outskirts of the forest of
Fontainebleau, and he has left painted souvenirs of all. He also
knew the forest quite as well. He had, on his wooden leg, explored
its densest fastnesses, and painted here, there, everywhere, the pools
to which the hunted stag stole out to drink, and where the wild birds
bathed—spots to which even the foresters rarely penetrated, and
where, when they did, they would point to the peculiar trail upon
the ground and remark, " The master has been here before us again."

So much has been written of the life of Diaz, that a note upon his death
should be of interest. This event occurred in the winter of 1876. His friend
and admirer, Albert Wolff, describes it in this magnificent apostrophe at the
termination of a sketch of his life :

" In 1876 Diaz felt himself seized with a malady of the chest that made all
work impossible ; he no longer possessed the resources for evoking the benefi-
cent sun by the magic of his color. Under the foggy sky of Paris he had no
wish to die ; the painter of the sun desired to have the sun as a witness of his
last agony. He took flight to Mentone, where, for the moment, he seemed
revived by the breath of a new life ; it was there that he painted his last pictures. Death surprised him at work, for it was necessary with this nature, still
rich in energy even in its final illness, to wrest the brushes from his hands and
break them. Vanquished at once in body and in spirit, Diaz made no further
resistance : without work, life had no seductions for him. From his bed of
anguish, through the open window, he saw the landscape swimming in sunlight, and the great enchanter died, contemplating, for the last time, the star
which had marshalled him to duty and to glory."

4

1 3 8 25

No. 35

JULES DUPRÉ

"The Little Farm"

8 x 10¼   *J.D. Tucker*

400

Cattle are drinking at a little pool which occupies the centre of the foreground. Trees dapple the water with shade, and in the middle ground a portion of the buildings of a farm is seen. The distance is marked in alternations of breezy light and shadow, under a sky in which roll fleecy masses of cloud. The time is midsummer and the hour midday.

It was the sale of his first Salon picture to the Duc de Nemours that laid the foundation for Jules Dupré's fortune and fame. Albert Wolff tells how, years after, when the duke had been long in political exile, till a turn in politics opened France to him again, Dupré called on him to pay his respects upon his arrival in Paris. The gallant young artist and the gallant young aristocrat of half a lifetime before faced each other, two fine, white-maned, time-seared old men, to whom fortune, with all her caprices, had not been altogether unkind. "Monseigneur," said the painter, "I have not forgotten that it was your Royal Highness who first made me an artist by encouraging me to be one." "And I have your picture yet," replied the prince. "Come, let us look at it;" and with the painter's arm in his he conducted him to the salon of the duchess, where hung the picture of that almost forgotten exhibition, still cloquent in its freshness and power of nature of the truth of the art that had created it. Dupré studied it for an instant in silence. The duke pressed his arm gently. "Your art, my friend," he said, "is more fortunate than you or I. It does not grow old."

No. 36

THEODORE ROUSSEAU

"The Farm, Sunset"

8 x 11

From the foreground a hill slopes upward to the middle plane, where its crest is crowned with the rambling structures of a farm shaded by trees. Over the brow of the hill, beyond the unseen low-land, a line of distant hills marks the horizon against a sky sodden with rain and inflamed with the lurid light of an angry sunset. The light of the sky reflects sullenly in a pool in the foreground, and the scud of the regathering storm blows in leaden vapors across the fading illumination of the inclement day.

The fierce battle for recognition, his repeated and deliberately unjust rejections at the Salon, and his long contest with poverty predisposed Rousseau to a frame of mind that would have rendered the works of a less courageous man melancholy and despairing in character. In him they aroused the poetical and reflective element latent in his blood. He was never happier than in the face of stormy sunsets, or of moonlit nights full of mystery and the vague charm of illimitable possibilities. He once wrote to a friend: "I saw a sunset to-night like the death of a madman, so full of terribly wild and dreamy forms, impossible of conception or description. I dare not paint it. I scarcely dare remember it." Within a decade after he penned these lines, he had solved the mystery of the mad sunset he dared not paint. He died insane.

No. 37

JULES DUPRÉ

" Banks of the Seine "

13 x 18

Perched upon a high bank a windmill rears its picturesque bulk against the sky. Near by is a farmhouse. The river divides the picture, and the farther bank rises in a high, sandy bluff. Blue masses of hills close the horizon in, and the sky, full of the movement of a coming storm, distributes great masses of shadow from its shifting clouds. A number of trading boats and freight barges lend life to the river, and moving figures make the shore busy. The composition possesses an almost panoramic vastness of space, but the effect is strikingly concentrated, the coloring rich, and the execution forcible to a degree not common even with the artist himself.

Albert Wolff considered Dupré not only one of the greatest landscape painters of the new era in France, but their precursor. While he was still painting on porcelain at Sèvres, he was spending his leisure time in the fields with sketch-book and pencil, and at eighteen years he had already become a young master. Landscape art was sunken in apparently hopeless artificiality when Dupré began to paint his pictures directly from nature. The young painter recognized the meaningless and worthless character of an art made up by rule in the studio, out of little scraps and sketches done from nature, after the fashion of the so-styled classical past ; and when it came his turn he began to paint not compositions or pictures, but bits of nature seized on the spot, with the skies gleaming, the clouds rolling, the waters flashing, the wind sweeping over the plains and rustling among the trees. People were at once astonished and charmed. They felt the truth he expressed, and accepted it, and the downfall of classical landscape began.

No. 38

ÉMILE VAN MARCKE

"At the Pool"

16100

18 x 22

In a shallow pool in the foreground some cattle have sought refreshment from the heat of the pasture. They are led by a handsome
cow, white with red markings, which stands in the middle of the
composition with its companions grouped behind it. A clump of
trees shades the pool; in the middle plane cattle are seen grazing in a
spacious meadow; and the sky is banked with clouds, brilliantly
lighted against a bright blue sky. The coloring is fresh, and the
treatment broad and vigorous. In composition and execution the
picture is one of the most characteristic of the artist's works.

1250

A native of Sèvres and a pupil of Troyon, Van Marcke came into an artistic
heritage upon his birth. His father was a landscape painter of merit, and his
mother a painter of flowers of a talent sufficiently pronounced to secure her a
Salon medal. An early marriage with the daughter of a chemist attached to
the Sèvres factories condemned him to nine years' servitude as a porcelain
painter. During this period he attracted the attention of Troyon, who weekly
visited Sèvres for a day to see his mother, who resided there. The master
advised the young porcelain painter to enter upon a more ambitious artistic
career, and in 1857 Van Marcke exhibited his first picture at the Salon. With
the death of Troyon, some ten years later, his follower succeeded to his place as
the first cattle painter of France. His earlier works exhibited to a considerable
extent the influence of his friend and master, but with the growth of his powers
came a style of his own. The only traces of Troyon one can discover in the
Van Marcke of to-day are a certain strength of form and breadth of effect, in
which the elder painter gloried, but which the younger artist qualifies with an
art and sentiment of his own, and which render all his work distinctive.

17850

No. 39

CONSTANT TROYON

"Strayed from the Herd"

16 x 20

Dispersed by a summer shower, a herd of cows have been separated over their pasturage. The squall is passing away, and the
rumblings of the thunder have followed the flashes of the lightning
into the wet and purple distance. One of the herd, a fine shapely
cow, is on the lookout for her companions. She occupies the centre
of the composition, and presents one of those types of animal life,
in her shapely symmetry of form and her beauty of markings, that
the artist studied so fondly and presented so well. The picture is
ripe and rich in color, and the treatment is indicative of the artist's
best period. It was one of the works which he preserved as most
representative of himself until his death, and was purchased at that
time from his studio.

No stronger or sturdier figure has existed in French art than Constant
Troyon. Born in 1810, the son of a porcelain painter, who wished him to continue the family trade, Troyon early broke away from irksome artificial labor
in the Sèvres factory, and went to nature for inspiration and the lessons of
truth in art. While by no means a slavish realist, he was ever an interpreter
of nature whose eye did not lose sight of his originals. His motives were
always picturesque, his effects generally magnificent in vastness and power,
his color fine, soberly rich and strong in harmonies which no false note ever
jarred, and his style never lacked the distinction of a master secure in his
knowledge and resources. Philip Gilbert Hamerton says truly of him that
"he had a more poetical mind than any other artist of the same class, and the
poetry of the fields has never been more feelingly interpreted than by him,"
and the "Dictionnaire Larousse" justly accords him an eternal place among the
masters of the *genre*.

No. 40

CARLETON WIGGINS

"The Approaching Storm"

Flower

23½ x 31½

The threatening weather has warned the grazing herd to assemble in the meadow, and they are now coming together. The sky, blackened with heavy banks of storm-clouds, is made the more sinister by the single streak of almost livid light left visible in it over the horizon. The intense darkness of a midsummer tempest shadows the earth, and in the deathlike calm that precedes the storm, nature awaits, shuddering, the bursting of the blast and the rending asunder of the clouds laden with waterspouts.

The lowlands of New Jersey, in the vicinity of New York City, have been more extensively favored by the landscape painter than by the painter of cattle. Mr. Wiggins was, perhaps, the pioneer in his walk of art to explore this fertile field of artistic suggestion and inspiration. The character of the scenery is individual as well as picturesque, and the variations of weather to which the district is subject lend it an additional charm to the artist. Every mood of nature may be studied in the meadows of the Hackensack, alternately made brilliant by sunlight and gloomed by sudden showers, basking in midsummer haze to-day and swept to-morrow by storms as brief in duration as they are sudden in their approach. These contrasts invest the subjects which the artist discovers with a certain dramatic quality which adds appreciably to their power and interest. It is not alone nature that is presented to his eye, but nature endowed with moods and caprices of her own, which furnish him with the foundation for works in which action and expression play an important part.

No. 41

GEORGES MICHEL

" The Forest Road "

27 x 35

A road leads out of the foreground into the forest, a forest such as one reads of in the life of Cartouche, and in the history of the " Bandits of Bondy." In the middle distance rises a bare and stony hillside, upon whose summit a lonely farmhouse is seen. A wan gray light illuminates the sky, piled up with clouds which darken over the horizon. A pallid gleam lights up the hillside. The foreground is in shadow, which, in the forest itself, deepens into positive gloom, fit atmosphere for the lurking footpad and the brigand, ambushed for the passing traveller, with his blunderbuss at full cock and murder and rapine in his heart.

The widow of Michel, when she supplied Sensier with the facts upon which he based his biography of her husband, related to him one curious incident. Early in his career, Michel made the acquaintance of the Baron d'Ivry, a very wealthy man and a passionate amateur of painting. Unfortunately the Baron's skill was not equal to his ambition, and on several occasions Michel added a touch to his pictures here and there to improve them. The Baron was charmed and proposed a partnership to him, in virtue of which Michel was to touch up his efforts at a fixed fee. This curious arrangement lasted for some years, during which Michel visited the house in secret and worked with his patron in a locked and guarded room. The Baron passed the retouched pictures off as his own works, and as he purchased everything that Michel finished on his own account as well, it is not unlikely that he may have enjoyed quite a reputation as an artist among his friends. But he was a generous paymaster and a sincere admirer of the painter. The Baron's ambition seems to have been to monopolize all of Michel's work ; and even when the State wished to purchase examples of it they were not available, as they had passed directly from the artist's easel to his patron's house.

No. 42

E. MEDARD

" A Change of Base "

30 x 36

An episode of that immortal siege of Paris out of which Frenchmen continue to extract artistic souvenirs of the glory of heroic defeat. A detachment of *gardes mobiles* have been driven in from work on the trenches at one point of the fortifications, and are executing a movement upon another base of defence. The excitement of the raw soldier shows itself in their ranks, and is in strong contrast to the disciplined steadiness and coolness of the regulars who form part of the main body. Artillery firing is seen in the distance. and here and there the ranks are broken by the fall of dead and wounded men.

Medard is one of the rare Frenchmen who have had the courage to paint war as anything but a national triumph of conquest. One of his most successful pictures was a " Retreat," showing a routed French army endeavoring to save its artillery over roads deep with snow and mire, with a multitude of sanguinary and realistic details. Medard's preference is for compositions comprising large bodies of troops and involving important strategic movements. He has studied the science of war as well as the art of painting war, and handles his battalions with military as well as picturesque skill. His personal experience in the service has thoroughly equipped him for his task, and many of his compositions are based on studies made by him during the annual reviews with which the French army is kept in military practice and perfected in discipline and precision. Accurate and painstaking in detail, his pictures have already taken high rank with his compatriots as permanent records of the stirring times which so completely revolutionized France in politics and spirit.

No. 43

W. C. BEAUQUESNE

"The Last Defence"

33⅝ x 46

It is the final stand of the forlorn hope. The army is in retreat.
Over roads where the mire is reddened with blood, the long trains of
ambulances heavy with mangled burdens, the lumbering artillery,
the color guard closing around a few tattered flags like the Spartan
legion at Thermopylæ, press through the gathering night, saved only
from the horrors of a rout by their confidence in that thin line of
steel that falls back only step by step between them and the pursuing
foe, fighting to the death behind burning cottages and broken walls
and in the ditches of abandoned and ruined farms, giving its own life
up that the lives of many may be saved for another cast of the deadly
dice of war. It is one of the heroic horrors of hopeless self-sacri-
fice that M. Beauquesne paints in this episode of thrilling anticipa-
tion, which in another moment will be a whirling chaos of flame and
blood and death.

Beauquesne belongs to the little army of military specialists in art whom the
Franco-Prussian war brought into existence. The conscription and the vol-
unteer service filled the ranks with art students and with painters who had
already taken their degrees. There was, indeed, an artistic legion enrolled for
service in the defence of Paris. At the end of the war the experiences of
the French artists in the field immediately began to reveal themselves in the
exhibitions. Beauquesne was one of the leaders in what may be called epi-
sodic battle painting. His pictures are all incidents of his campaigns, noted
down at the time in his sketch-book and executed later with a dash and vigor
which show that the painter's reminiscences have lost none of their pristine
fire. They make no pretension to the rigid accuracy of detail that characterizes De Neuville and Detaille, but stand apart as strong, individual impressions
of a time calculated to impress itself deeply upon any receptive mind. Character, action, and a clear story vividly told are their main characteristics.

No. 44

CHARLES ÉMILE JACQUE

"The Two Shepherds"

M. Tallman

20915

27 X 21

540

They repose upon the turf at the edge of a little wood, the master indulging in a doze while his dog keeps watchful guard upon his charges. There is no fear of the sheep going astray under such vigilant sentryship. The flock grazes about, content to browse and nibble where the fare is good, without ambition to go further afield, although the beaten path invites them to an exploration of the mysteries of the grove. The foreground is occupied by a pool, which darkens under the reflection of a gray sky, portentous of the approach of autumn with its shrewd winds and chilling rains, that will drive flock and shepherds under shelter in a few weeks more.

When, after years of absence from the Salon, Jacque sent to that of 1888 two compositions worthy of his best period, the French hailed the occasion almost as a national triumph. One enthusiastic publisher promptly purchased the right to have his principal composition etched. Both pictures were purchased before the Salon was fairly opened. The triumph of the veteran, among his hen-coops and his sheep-stables far away from the noisy town, was as complete as triumph could be. The artist seems to have found life happy in his rural retreat during his later years. His simple peasant neighbors regard him with a cross between reverence for his genius—which they cannot understand—and fear of him as a madman because of his practice of collecting worthless things for use as models. Once he found a shepherd about to drown a poor old sheep-dog that had outlived its usefulness. He purchased the doomed brute, and till it died a natural death it was his constant companion and a regular figure in his pictures. At another time a peasant was preparing to smash up a broken and weather-stained old wheelbarrow for firewood. Jacque secured it at the price of a new one. His studio was an open market for wornout tools and tattered blouses and broken sabots. No wonder that the frugal rural mind sees in these extravagances the vagaries of a disordered brain.

21455

No. 45

ALEXANDRE GABRIEL DECAMPS

"The Tempest"

24 x 26   *J. Wolfe*

It has been a day of showers. The earth is saturated with moisture, and the ground is puddled and cut into runnels with the rains.
As the day has declined the weather has grown worse, until it has
acquired the bluster of one of those tempests that roar their fury
through the night, wreaking wrecks in the darkness. The huntsman
and his dog plod wearily homeward after a spoiled day's sport,
through roads of mire, buffeted by angry gusts from the savage sky.
Desolation blows across the landscape like a ghost. The gale
whistles amid the verdure of the young oaks, and wrestles fiercely
with the sturdy branches of the veteran stem that guards the roadside, and that to-morrow may be prone, one of the first victims of the
tempest's wanton wrath.

Decamps made his public start in art as one of the satirists of the period of
the Restoration in France, whose famous lithographed caricatures had such
an influence on the politics of the day. The Greek struggle for independence
attracted him to the East, but he abandoned patriotism for art when he found
himself face to face with the picturesque life of Asia-Minor. His first exhibits
in the Salon of 1831 were of subjects from the Orient, handled so originally,
and with such vigor of effect and color, that they scored a prodigious success,
and ranked him at once with the foremost painters of the new school. His
ambition was to be a great historical painter, however, and while he scored
successes with his biblical and historical pictures he never touched the standard he aspired to. He retired into the country, where he gave himself up to
the chase and to painting the scenes about him. He cultivated no intimacies,
and sought the solitude of the forest, with his dogs, at the first threat of a visi-
tor. The failure of his great dream undoubtedly oppressed him to his tragic
end, and he died, in spite of his fame and the fortune it brought, a soured and
misanthropic man.

5

No. 46

PIERRE-ETIENNE-THEODORE ROUSSEAU

"The Goatherd"

Béraud

19 x 13½

At the foot of a magnificent old oak tree, sturdy still in spite of the blasting assaults of the lightning and the inroads of natural decay, a goatherd reposes on the grass while his flock graze about him. Although he gives the title to the picture, its interest centres in the splendid portrait of the monarch of the forest which forms its majestic centre, and which is surely one of the noblest studies of a great landmark of nature ever painted. The background is in keeping with the old oak tree itself, lonely and wild, full of the charm of the remoter forest where nature reigns supreme and man finds only incidental tolerance.

Rousseau was the son of a tailor, and entered upon the study of art with the sanction of his parents. He, it is told, secured their consent by secretly procuring colors and brushes, and painting a view of the village church and graveyard of Montmartre, in which district he had begun sketching with the pencil as a schoolboy. Rousseau speedily revolted at the stiff and artificial style of landscape then alone in vogue, and turning his back on classicism went forth to nature as a school. He explored the remoter and more lonely and savage sections of France, living for months in the mountains and the forests, and making everywhere those close and highly finished studies upon which his future style was founded. In the same manner he explored the vicinity of Paris for material. Sensier describes him as spending his days outside the barriers, sketching, and hurrying home after dark to paint by candle-light in his studio. He began to attract attention in the Salon in 1830, and one of his first pictures was purchased by the Duc d'Orleans for a good price. The Government also made a bid for this picture for the National collection. The beginning was certainly auspicious for him. But political changes affected the *personnel* of the Salon jury, and filled it with his enemies. The silent and thoughtful bachelor married a woman subject to fits of incurable and violent derangement. With the insults and injuries of his enemies to goad him on the one hand, and the horrors of a perpetual domestic inferno to rack him on the other, Rousseau, during the most glorious period of his life, endured the torments of a rock-bound Prometheus. He staggered under the burden till it bore him down, and died, a paralytic, with an unbalanced mind, while the mad wife survived him.

No. 47

J. L. E. MEISSONIER

"On the Lookout"

8 x 5½

In a modest public house interior, of the middle of the last century, a gentleman stands at his window watching for some passing object of interest in the street below. He leans at ease against the angle of the wall in which the window is recessed. His right hand is in his breeches pocket. His left has just removed a long-stemmed clay pipe from his mouth and holds it at the level of his breast. He wears a black coat over a red waistcoat rather negligently buttoned, red breeches, gray stockings, and black shoes with silver buckles. His black hat is on his head, and his shirt of lawn, unadorned with lace, shows at the throat and wrists. Behind him is a chair from which he has apparently risen in his impatience at the tardiness of the other party, to the appointment of which he is the first upon the scene.

The man at the window has ever been a favorite subject with Meissonier. He has painted him in the costumes of a dozen periods, doing twenty different things, but never, in any sense, as a repetition. The master is not a producer of replicas. He frequently essays the exploitation of every side of an idea, but if he paints ten " Smokers " each is a different smoker, smoking and thinking and looking differently from the others. So it is with his men at the window. In the face of one we read cupidity awaiting the settlement of a debt; in another passion anticipating desire with fever-flushed face; in another the indifferent friend whom a friend has summoned in order to confide his woes to him. Such, perhaps, is the gentleman of this picture. Certainly his expression is not serious enough for a duelist, or anxious enough for a lover whose mistress keeps him tarrying at the tryst. He is simply rath... bored. It is a bright day outside. Paris is all abroad. What folly for a fellow to dry himself up with tobacco smoke when there are pretty faces in the garden of the Palais Royal, and witty words being bandied at the club. M. Meissonier has the gift of making you think for his heroes, and this, no doubt, is what he wishes us to think for this one.

0 3 o *Ų*

No. 48

JEAN FRANÇOIS MILLET

"The Seamstress"

16 x 13

2 1 0 0

In a kitchen interior a woman is seen in profile, at full length, seated on a wicker-bottomed chair. She is sewing, with her face turned down upon her work. She wears a gray cloth bodice, with a blue cotton apron over a brown dress; a white cap on her head, and a white collar at her neck, giving special relief to her face against the background. The color is quiet but strong, and the pose of the figure is characterized by that modest grace which Millet so well knew how to give to the least complete as well as the most highly finished representation of the female form, however garbed. The expression of intentness upon her task, and the suggestion of movement in the seamstress's hands, are extremely characteristic. The picture is a close study from life, finished with care.

The pedigree of this admirable example of the master, at his best period, is given in a letter upon the back. The picture was purchased from a private collection in Paris, in December, 1883, by P. F. Rudell, an American artist at that time prosecuting his studies in Europe. Although the inherent evidences of its authenticity were indubitable, Mr. Rudell added the crown to them by submitting the picture to Mme. Millet. She recognized it at once, and recalled clearly the circumstances under which it had been painted by her husband.

29 30

No. 49

FRANÇOIS MILLET

2 9730

"The Haystack"

21½ x 29½

They are building up the great haystack, the pride of the farm.
It has arisen tier on tier, until now the man who stands upon the
loaded haywagon must reach his forkful up to a man on a ladder
before it can be got to those who are levelling and packing the
towering top. Two wagons keep the stackers supplied. The
horses, worn out by a hard and long day's toil, doze in their traces
or nibble a surreptitious mouthful from the stack. The field is
nearly bare. But a few more sheaves remain for removal. The
peaceful country reaches into a remote distance, and behind the stack
a portion of the farm buildings is seen, all bathed in the glory of a
golden late afternoon.

320

The commanding genius of the great Millet impressed itself indelibly upon
two members of his family. One is his brother, who after the death of their
mother and the breaking up of the family came to live and study with him at
Barbizon, and who is still alive. The work of this Millet is neither strong nor
original, but it is full of suggestions of his brother's earlier style. François
Millet, the son, has advanced much farther. In many features, the selection of
subjects and their treatment especially, he shows the influence of his father's
art, and certain of his peasant figures in pastel present a striking similarity to
his parent's. It is in oil that he is most original and individual, and while he
selects rural scenes, animated by figures, he treats them with a sentiment and a
feeling for color that invest them with a peculiar charm of their own. In spite
of the burden of a great name, the younger Millet occupies a position of
marked personal and artistic consideration in France, though it is only of very
recent years that his works have begun to find their way to the United States.

5

29450

No. 50

ALPHONSE DE NEUVILLE

"The Vanguard"

20 x 15½

J. Wolf

29450

The army is on the move. Through peaceful fields, where the harvest has been stacked despite the tumult of war, the vanguard advances with a sharp lookout for signs of the enemy. Each man clutches his bridle with a hand that is ready to respond to the first warning of voice and eye. The horses themselves seem to participate in the general spirit of caution and watchfulness. It would require but a word to transform this battalion, stringing along through the plain with the measured movement of a monstrous snake, into a serried front of flashing steel, with every heart throbbing for action, and every hand armed for the work of death.

"De Neuville," says Mr. Henry Bacon in his "Parisian Art and Artists," "was first known as an illustrator, being one of the best in France, and his drawings were eagerly sought by publishers, abroad as well as at home. This early training gave him such facility of drawing, such readiness of composition, that when he entered the wider field of painting, he had but to add color to an almost perfect talent, and stood at once foremost among his competitors." De Neuville trusted nothing in his pictures to chance. He used models for everything. When he went on his summer vacations, his *valet-de-chambre* and his cook accompanied him, dressed as soldiers, and posed between the execution of their domestic duties for their master's use. As an illustration of his closeness of observation and study, it is told that while painting his celebrated picture, "The Last Cartridge," he caused a running fire of musketry to be discharged by his models, in order that he might catch the spirit even of the smoke and fix it on his canvas. De Neuville was one of the very few men whom Delacroix admitted to intimacy in his declining years. His door was open to him when it was barred to all others, and the heroic veteran of the days of the French revolution in art was, to the last, a guide, counsellor, and friend to the young artist of these newer and vastly altered times.

No. 51

3 2 4 5 0

NARCISSE VIRGILE DIAZ (DE LA PEÑA)

" Early Autumn, Forest of Fontainebleau "

Ur.

20 X 26

2 4 5 0

The first light touch of the frost has commenced to invest the forest in the livery of autumn. Among the lingering greens of the ripened summer time, the russets of the fall are stealing in. Overhead the sky is blue, with the intense blue that is unmarred by mists. The forest pool still refreshes the birds that have not yet commenced their southward flight, and in the coverts of fern the hare and the woodhen yet find refuge, undisturbed by anticipations of the coming snow. The sunlight is still warm and mellow that pours in through the opening in the wood, and sends exploring rays among the trees, touching their mossy trunks with glints of light, and giving to a green or red leaf here and there the flash of an emerald or a ruby.

When Albert Wolff was introduced to Diaz for the first time, he relates that he remarked to the painter that he owned one of his pictures, which he described. Diaz listened with interest, and requested permission to call on his new acquaintance and examine the work. Next morning he made the visit. His host noted that he viewed the picture with repressed emotion. It represented a baby asleep in a cradle, and its mother sleeping in a chair beside it, with the sunlight flooding in through an open window. After some moments Diaz bluntly asked his host if he would sell the picture. The latter offered to give it to him. Finally they arranged to exchange it for another, and Diaz said : " You have given me greater pleasure than I can describe. This woman and child are my family. I painted them from nature, as they are, one summer afternoon. For years the picture was part of the furniture of my bedroom, but one day, when I was desperately hard up, a dealer who came along looking for bargains offered me one hundred and fifty francs for it. I offered him anything else, but he had set his mind on just this picture, and I finally sold it to him. It was like carrying off a part of my heart, but hunger knows no sentiment. From that day till this I had not seen or heard of it, and I certainly never expected to recover it again. Now I have recovered a part of my youth with it, and you are the good genius who restores it to me."

3 4 0

68   THE BOWNE COLLECTION.

No. 52

J. C. CAZIN

"The Hour of Rest and Peace"

W. J. Taylor   23 x 29

The last gleam lingers in a sky over which the clouds that carry
evening showers drift in rifted masses. The landscape is veiled in
the transparent shadow of early twilight. The fields are dim, and the
vapor rising from the streams commences to obscure without oblit-
erating the distant hills. The village road, passing across the foreground, loses itself among the houses and gardens in the middle
plane. Over the fields, in one of the cottages, an evening lamp
already gleams in the window. It is the hour of rest and peace, not
only in its title, but also in the exquisite tenderness of touch and
poetry of sentiment with which the artist has fixed it on the canvas.

Cazin, of all the landscape painters of the day, is the one who approaches
Corot nearest in spirit. Their styles are entirely different, but they see nature
with the same eyes, and the differences in their individual renditions of her are
largely a matter of temperament. Cazin's touch possesses a certain bold
frankness and decision that give force and vigor to his most delicate experiments in color, and although his taste inclines him to experiment upon well-
defined lines it is to be noted that his variety in the field he has made his own
is as infinite as that of nature herself. It is his faculty of comprehending and
his power of translating the subtlest inflections of color and atmosphere and
the finest variations of light and shade, that invests his simplest subjects with
the importance of the most ambitious pictures that he paints. They are all
notes scored from the great harmonies of nature, and in none of them does the
artist strike a discord. Cazin, at one time claimed with rapture by the impres-
sionists, is in fact the leader in the higher realism of landscape painting of our
time, and is as yet but at the threshold of his triumphs.

No. 53

J. B. C. COROT

"The Road to the Sea"

36 x 42

3 5 9 5 0

2 3 0 6

It is morning. Over the crown of a hillside, down which a road descends, the roofs of village houses are seen. The hillside, the road, the broken ground, brushwood, and trees, which constitute the foreground, are all in shadow, but full of variety and form, delicately defined and suggested, and constituting a harmonious and finely balanced mass of subdued color against the luminous sky. The figure of a fisherman in the road lends the one needed point of vitality to the picture, which is a remarkably perfect example of natural composition, rendered by the artist with the greatest frankness and the finest appreciation of its subtleties. The color and handling indicate the work to be a product of Corot's strongest period.

It is a part of the legend of Corot's life that he was sixty years of age before he sold a picture. He is said to have remarked to a friend on this occasion, "I have sold a picture at last. It is a pity. It breaks my collection." His expansive benevolence, however, gave him ample use for the money, when the demand for his works did begin. He had, upon the death of his father, come into an income of 40,000 francs. The principal would revert, upon his death, to relations. He scarcely touched even the interest, allowing it to accumulate for the benefit of his heirs. He lived in inexpensive lodgings, and disbursed the enormous sums his pictures brought him in among his needy friends and brother artists. When Daumier was about to be turned out of the house in which he had lived many years, Corot purchased it and presented it to him. His friend accepted the gift, saying simply, "You are the only man I esteem sufficiently to be able to accept such a favor from without a blush." A short time before his death, he closed a very large transaction with a wealthy merchant. When the latter settled for the pictures he had purchased, Corot passed

3 8 2 5 0

him back ten notes of a thousand francs each. "Take care of these for me," he said, "and hand one every year for ten years to the widow of my friend Millet." On another occasion a painter friend called on him to borrow 5,000 francs. Corot was in a bad humor that morning, and replied that he had not the money. The moment the dejected man left the room, Corot's conscience smote him. He stripped off his blouse, gathered up from his drawer the required sum, and hurried after his friend to beg his pardon and force the loan upon him. This drawer of Corot's was famous. In it, mixed with sketchbooks, letters, squeezed-out paint tubes, and the like. was sometimes as much as 100,000 francs—the sinking fund on which the master drew for his benevolences.

No. 54
ÉMILE LAMBINET

" A Nook of the Seine "

26 x 36

38250

The foreground is occupied by one of those placid and almost tide-less backwaters of the Seine, in which the water-lily carpets the flood and walls of rushes provide coverts for the crane. Against the sky quivering with light, the delicate outlines of the alders and willows build up in the middle plane a picturesque mass of verdure, whose note of color, indefinite yet strong, accentuates the luminosity of the atmosphere itself. The picture is another solution of the problem which the artist continually sets himself—the problem of painting light at its highest pitch, penetrating, dazzling, and vibrant with the pulsations of life.

550

Lambinet, a native of the country of the Seine, will pass into the history of art as its chief historian. Although he has found subjects at a distance, the greater number of his works are transcripts of the nature amid which he was born. It has been said of him, as was said of Daubigny in regard to the Oise, that he has made the Seine immortal, so that if its channel should ever run dry it would still exist and be perpetuated by his art. The subjects selected by Lambinet are invariably simple in character. His pictures are, in fact, successive experiments in the painting of light, keyed to its highest pitch, as it might be in rivalry with nature herself. No essay is too daring for him, and his invariable success with these has presented the world with a succession of the most brilliant canvases, in which the modesty of the composition and the simple adjustment of the color scheme are lost in the radiant brightness with which he endows the picture, as if he had mastered the secret of the sun and fixed it on his palette.

38800

No. 55

38800

CHARLES-FRANÇOIS DAUBIGNY

"The Time of Apple Blossoms"

fi. Lg, Sione — 33 x 62

The orchard is in blossom, and all the landscape is green with the refreshing verdure of young spring. The branches of the willows have the delicate contour of plumes, and the turf shows the varying shade and color of green plush in the soft and hazy light. Never so happy as in painting the re-awakening of the year at its most beautiful period, the master painter of the Oise is at home here in one of the most felicitously achieved of his favorite subjects. It is a true idyll of the springtime, instinct with color, light, the richness of mounting sap in branch and grass, the fatness of the generous earth, renewing itself under a breeze that has the refreshing stimulus of new wine.

It was Théophile Gautier, in his "Abécédaire du Salon de 1861," who charged Daubigny with being too readily content to fix his first impression upon canvas, and permit it to pass as complete. This was, to a certain extent, a just criticism, but Gautier did not give the painter credit for the enormous vitality and power, the quality of suggested completeness, that he could put in the slightest impression, no matter how small its size. Nor did he score to his credit those great canvases which, when the subject especially appealed to him, he fondled with so loving and patient a hand. The river Oise and its banks were Daubigny's chief sketching fields. He kept a boat fitted up for long excursions, with food and wine and cooking apparatus, and in it he drifted, worked, ate, and even slept, as long as the season permitted it. "The Time of Apple Blossoms" is one of his subjects of the Oise country, which, painted at a time when his smaller works were popular, he used to say he did for the satisfaction of doing them. His ambition, indeed, was "to paint pictures that would not sell," and he thus, unconsciously, produced his greatest and most important works. His devotion to his art is said to have been the direct cause of Daubigny's death. Living and working so much upon the water, often in seasons of rain and fog, he contracted a rheumatism which rendered his end one of cruel agony. His last thought, according to his biographers, was of his art, and he died with the name of his beloved friend Corot on his lips.

42000

Bowne

No. 56

42000

CARLETON WIGGINS

"Among the Rushes"

30 x 56

8 00

A sedate white cow, grazing amid the salt grass pastures of Long Island, has halted in a rushy pool among the sand-dunes to survey her surroundings. The poise of the animal and her expression of attention are admirably conveyed. The sea-breeze stirs the clouded sky and blows the bending reeds. The sunlight has a sharp gleam, and the water ripples under the breath of the wind. A sense of wide space and free, fresh air characterizes the whole composition and makes it vivid in its realistic strength.

Born in Turners, N. Y., in 1848, Carleton Wiggins was, until recently, identified with the small but able art colony of Brooklyn, where he had his studio. He acquired his first experiences in art as a student of the National Academy of Design, and later as a pupil of H. Carmienke, but his strongest development is the result of some years of observation, study, and experiment in Europe. He first exhibited at the National Academy in 1870, and in 1881 his first exhibit at the Paris Salon secured him the indorsement of French critics. While essentially a painter of cattle, Mr. Wiggins is also known as the author of landscapes of rare quality and beauty of color and of feeling. He stands at the head of the younger school of cattle painters in America.

42800

42800

No. 57

AUGUSTE HAGBORG

" The Mussel Gatherer "

1500

50 x 32   *M. L. Bowne*

Interrupted in the mussel harvest by the rising of the tide, a
sturdy and comely fishermaiden has turned her face landward, and
measures the wide beach with long, strong strides, bearing her well-
filled basket as lightly as a child might carry a toy. The coast
reaches away behind her in a long perspective of shore and sand ;
the sea is gray and full of movement under the gray and windy sky,
while the screaming gulls, cleaving the air in clamorous and uneasy
flight, seem to predict the rising gale which will follow the rising
tide.

Hagborg is one of those men of the North of whom Sainte-Beuve once wrote:
" They sing to us, with their brushes or their pens as it may be, tender and
simple romances of lives which wrest contentment from the surging sea and
the swirling snow." A certain seriousness and gravity dominate the spirit of
Hagborg, but never predispose him to melancholy or gloom. Life is serious
in his eyes, but full of brightness too. Although born in Sweden and grounded
in his art at the National School of the Arts, he really graduated in Paris, under
Palmaroli, so that some of the lighter and airier elements of the genius of the
South are grafted on his Northern temperament. These show themselves in his
method of treating his subjects, of which " The Mussel Gatherer " is a superior
example. In choice of subjects themselves he remains faithful to his father-
land.

44300

No. 58

GEORGES MICHEL

"Montmartre"

31 x 50

Bennett

44300

1050

From an elevation which provides an irregular line of foreground, we look down upon the plain of Montmartre as it was at the commencement of the century. Over the vast expanse of what is now one of the most populous parts of Paris and its suburbs, the lights and shadows of the storm are at sinister play. Overhead the clouds are blown in tormented masses by the blast. The wan light of the tempestuous day gives ghastly prominence to a little village on the plain, with its few houses and its windmills, which latter were Montmartre's trademark in the past.

Montmartre was Michel's favorite and chosen sketching ground. Every afternoon, at a fixed hour, he would put up the shutters of his little curiosity shop in Paris, and in company with his wife post off to the region of windmills and quarries, to paint. Summer or winter, foul weather or fair, the curious pair were still to be seen somewhere about the district, and the titanic energy with which Michel worked resulted in the production of a great number of pictures of Montmartre, which have now become priceless. Few equalled in size or importance this example, which is of unusual dimensions and care of execution for him. Michel, although he began life as a painter, and prospered latterly, made no pretence of living by his art. He accumulated a little money at a petty trade, which he had established for his son, who died, when the father continued the business, and put his pictures away as he painted them. He died in contented and comfortable poverty in 1843, in his own house, just after the movement in art which he had begun had been taken up by the greater masters, Corot, Rousseau, Diaz, Daubigny, and Millet.

Paris

45350

No. 59

MEINDERT HOBBEMA

"A Dutch Landscape"

45 350

W. a. Taylor

34 X 43

This is a landscape from the district of Drenthe, where Hobbema found the material for most of his pictures of this character, while Gueldres supplied him with those bustling streams with primitive water mills that constitute the other variation of his art. Here he gives us a road, entering into a scattered oak wood which occupies the foreground. In the middle distance some trees, the outriders of the forest, are seen, and the distance is a great champaign, made joyous by the golden rays of the sun which the painter loved so well to depict. A wagon drawn by two horses and filled with peasants is entering the wood, and at the roadside some woodcutters pause at their work to give the passers-by good cheer. The picture is a remarkably strong and superior example of the master, and in matchless condition of preservation.

Of Hobbema's personal history, little is known. He was born in Amsterdam, was a friend of Jacob van Ruysdael, and like Ruysdael was almost ignored by his contemporaries. He devoted himself altogether to copying the nature that surrounded him, and although endowed with less taste and less poetic feeling than Ruysdael he copied nature more closely. M. Henri Havard says, " Whilst the former produces his effects by mysterious undefined light and shade, the latter, on the contrary, illumes his pictures with brilliant sunlight, which, finding its way through the foliage of his great trees, gives an idea of contentment and joy. Whilst the one chooses the twilight hours when nature is shrouded with a kind of veil, the other prefers the setting sun in all its brilliancy, warming the grassland by its rays and making it golden with its reflection. As regards excellence of execution, these two painters may be classed together ; and if the brush of Ruysdael appears to be softer and more supple, that of Hobbema is more decided in coloring and more robust in execution."

It was not until 1739, a century after his birth, that Hobbema's name began to figure in the sales catalogues. His works are rare. The museums of Berlin, Brussels, and Amsterdam are almost the only ones on the continent which possess any of them. There is but one in the Pinakothek at Munich. The best examples, according to M. Havard, are to be found in private collections and particularly in England, the Dulwich gallery owning an important work. "High as their merit is," says this authority, "it is quite as much to their scarcity that we may attribute the high prices at which they are valued at the present day."

AMERICAN ART ASSOCIATION,
MANAGERS.